SAINT TWIN

Library and Archives Canada Cataloguing in Publication

Burgoyne, Sarah, author
Saint twin / Sarah Burgoyne.

Poems.
ISBN 978-1-77126-113-5 (paperback)

I. Title.

PS8503.U73715S35 2016 C811'.54 C2016-901476-2

Editor for the press: Stuart Ross
Typesetting & cover design: Stuart Ross
Author photo: Eloise Bergen

The publication of *Saint Twin* has been generously supported by
the Canada Council for the Arts and the Ontario Arts Council.

Mansfield Press Inc.
25 Mansfield Avenue, Toronto, Ontario, Canada M6J 2A9
Publisher: Denis De Klerck
www.mansfieldpress.net

SAINT TWIN

SARAH BURGOYNE

Mansfield Press

deep below the ice the trout
are perfect
   —John Thompson

Hooves! Hooves!
   —Samuel Beckett

CONTENTS

AN EAGLE FLEW IN THE SUN AGAIN
BUT IT DIDN'T MEAN THE SAME

i've seen loss bless you
i felt everything but envy

yet here you are at the edge of the sea
with nothing worth reporting

nothing to replace
your memories of the farm
the nervous thousand-palmed birches
the fortress your sister made of rocks

nothing will suffice
the sun sets on only a few trees
and the great grey owl flies headlessly on

the days go by
and every vision
comes to nothing

you left the ocean behind
but the river could have led you
through the valley

AT THE POTTER'S HOUSE

I blew out the candle to see the holy smoke.

The leaves of your lettuce

were beautiful in the half-full shadows.

I will not let the beans boil over.

All life I loved the Holy Missus most.

The first myths about fruit becoming

enormous. Then it's time to find a new gift.

All very real, like birthdays.

P7jamas were good enough, so why

the dead face? Take my hand, John.

I will abandon my whole existence

eating a bowl of peaches.

AT LEAST BEST, IT DIDN'T MATTER.

What was at issue was not so much what had been lost, as what hadn't been felt. A sum's worth of nothing new, always new, with newness fleeting. The way the vine hung in quieter moments such as after dinner, pawing the looker's pent-up soul, which was nothing. Not even those more delirious moments all the while awaiting. It wasn't the whole point. The night ships of anger, sailing toward. The furthest station heart-swamped with nineteen. Visions as well as beer would run out, as would the days of winter months, the many it took, and on.

ALLOW ME, WHEN I LOOK, TO MARVEL AT YOU

above us the stars made pictures of our bodies
we couldn't understand   you were looking
for affirmation   i was looking

for a boulder flat enough to lie on

your father   the morning he disappeared
ground the coffee beans   as usual

the priest read from his book

prepare chains
the land is full of bloodshed
and the city   full of violence

after the funeral you said you wanted to be buried
under white cloth   be found by some women
and appear before your friends the next day
                              altered
and calling for fish

in my dreams the thief fails to arrive

the dragon   with its seven heads
turns them all away

A NEW CAKELAND

for N.P.

When John sat at the bar
said, "Let's order a tall one."
The building dropped
left a big big hole.

That's a perfect, right?
Fell to again and positively
walked up H street.
You forget things for reasons.

Hidden twin of a first spirit, eat your cream
and soft green peppercorns
and I'll go rob the creek.

I'll show you how we grow
thin and strong
like a trout raised by nurses.

LOVE, PLEASE DO SO AT THE SELF

I myself walked myself to the funeral home, splitting ears and hairs along the way. "Go with the grain of the soap," she always said. So I journeyed deep into the mould, and ended up on a Chinese mountain. It was easier to see this way, said the rock, pointing up. A deer passed by, wearing its skeleton costume on the inside, and my heart filled up my heart up.

Putting the bread on the cheese was never the same as putting the cheese on the bread. Being a cook is easy! said the Pescatarian. "The oval look of your eyes makes me beautiful thoughts." If you choose to borrow these thoughts, I won't mind. They are a fish in my skull, shedding spangles all over, why my teeth are gold. In fact, if you look beneath my skin suit, my whole bones are gold.

"Better go see the chicken gods again." It was always enough to get a coffee, at least. The best on Sundays, when it was free and we were free to be free also. To be free also was the name of a song that was popular once and then banned, among other song names and types of winks. Did you see that bird looking straight at you? the elephant asked. I am impressed by your hairdo. Do I even need to say it?

Something made sense at my self yesterday and the gates of my sad were stopped. Did you imagine writing this on the bathroom stall? If you do not require this story, please leave it on the shelf. P.S.—That old suitcase? I opened it, and there was nothing in it but more suitcase. Next time, look behind the mirror for your suitcase's reflection.

THAT CHASE WITH THE HOUNDS FOR THE UNATTAINABLE MEANING OF THE WORLD

In the event that disaster strikes, if disaster is even what one would call it, and in case all forms of public transport stop, granted that the ground remains intact, then it is good that one would walk, provided one has two working legs, or even just one, so long as the prosthetic other is sound, unless of course it breaks along the way, given that one does not have a spare, and the fastening of the spare to the body would be simple enough, on the condition that one does not even need one (or two), and even if one does, well, for the purpose of walking when disaster strikes, one has no other option.

IT IS BITTER TO SING IN PRAISE OF THE MIND

the leaves on the pond
broke records that year

for turning the colour of fire
all at the same time

across the water   children shrieked at gulls
while the sun bore westward
across the sound

today   you are a child too

sometimes   when you see a bird
it is flying straight for your head

A LITTLE BLACK HOUSE ON THE SEASHORE
(A Poem in Four Stories)

It was the final note. Steam moving up the way of snow. Had I been here before? asked the crow at wit's end. A stone rolled ahead of us, to where the kayakers had capsized in the rapids. Someone cackled and we lost all the candy. Take me to the nearest valley so I can make declarations! So there we went and a joke was made. It was not so funny after all, but at least we were moved.

A GRAVE BESIDE THE BAD KIDS

You are floating by like sill-flies

on some holy breath. A small cough

over a pretty dress.

I don't think, friend, so.

John, you nestle in the parking lots

of God's love. It took this

long to become a friend of saints.

Moses knew the best places

to look and not look. Should've asked.

With this intention, I set out whenever I felt inclined so as to practice walking great distances, usually passing from the east side of Montréal to the west and back, sometimes over the mountain, sometimes crossing The Main at the mountain's east side. Since paranoia is conducive to poetics, owing to its derivative hyper-sensitivity, in the hope that such activity and experience of the senses would produce superior metaphors (while at the same time skeptical of this result due to the sound advice of my mother), I set out walking to the end that perhaps something noteworthy would be written during one such peripatetic hypothetical-disaster emergency drill with this (disaster) in mind. In other words, for fear that catastrophe could strike any moment and because of my mother's advice to "sois prête" inasmuch as one could be prepared (considering the element of surprise), in order to survive as best one could (given that of course disaster strikes). Since I had to consider all these things, in view of my own survival on the planet, while I did like walking and did not have a dog or some other creature to inspire the act, it took on a new imperative: lest we disaster.

TO THE MASTERS OF OUR YOUTH, GREETINGS

the last days of a person's life are the same
as the first   someone says at the party   one mountain
will always stay hidden behind another

and the orange
unround moon

will light up a field
that knows nothing of your goings

meanwhile in your apartment
the zanzibar gem grows a new arm
and someone spills a drink

to take things seriously means to avoid

the idiotic glass
that fills or empties
according to outlook

the stain on your shirt
your last coat of arms

means the same as the first

A LITTLE BLACK HOUSE ON THE SEASHORE

Over pancakes the other day, John asked for a new way of organizing sheep and goats. "Impossible," I said, flipping batter. But he kept thinking out loud: "Horns can't be the only things distinguishing people." I agreed but burned a flapjack. Everything looks alike, covered in blueberries. Someone must always be hungry.

FOR I BELIEVED IN THE EXISTENCE OF A LAST DOOR

1.

this is all that I have learned
god made us plain and simple
but we have made ourselves very complicated

2.

i have discovered only this
god made human beings for righteousness
but they seek out many alternatives

3.

see this alone i found
that god made man upright
but they have sought out many schemes

ANOINTING MY OWN HEAD WITH MY OWN OIL

He did not open his mouth
after bearing all the sins.
I say! These are like the days
of ____! So now I have sworn
not angry to be with you.

Probably you will forget
your youthful shame.
You will lengthen some ropes
with snakes, the cool way.
And bless a young seventh
wife. (Sing, O barren women.)

But who can speak
of imaginary descendants?
The ice cools the glass
inside and out.

THE ONIONS IN THE STORE REFUSE ALL
COMPARISONS, ESPECIALLY TO PEARLS

when the alley floods
the short walk from the corner store to our home
lengthens

inside the upright lamp makes a mockery
of the houseplants

and a spider escapes
its jar

you say that each moment it isn't open
the door becomes more closed

i say the light always hangs from a cord and the cord
is always connected

to a pillar of silver fire

In other words, walking became a common pastime for me and my twin who, as a dog raises its hair, also felt the prickling of disaster. Walking in Montréal was loved by everybody, including myself and my twin. For one thing, certain streets are brimming with people who, like us, enjoy walking in particular, whether or not they are sound. As an illustration, one night we (my twin and I and our sister) were walking up Sainte-Catherine (east to be sure), when a young man approached to examine my sister's bicycle in detail. In this case, that of the young man, something was not quite right, or sound—namely, he kept asking the price of the bicycle of our sister when indeed the bicycle was not for sale. My sister, to demonstrate the bicycle was not for sale, kept pointing to herself saying "c'est la mienne" and for this reason we thought for certain the young man would understand, chiefly through the relaying of the message through plain speech (that being: "it's mine"), and would not need the superfluous gesticulation to emphasize the simple fact that the bicycle was not for sale. The act of my sister making energetic motions with her limbs was merely to put it another way. Truly, for him to repeat the question "c'est combien?" (that is to say, "how much for your bicycle?") was disheartening. To clarify that it was not for sale, with attention to his current derangement, was useless. To explain the bicycle was not for sale to a small dog or an orange cone by all means seemed to make just as much sense. Surely, to enumerate the quantity of refusals to sell the bicycle would be boring for "tout le monde."

A LITTLE BLACK HOUSE ON THE SEASHORE

Lately, it has been house after house on fire, and cardamom pastries for some. Who will rescue the pretty vegetables, I wonder. A collar emerged from the cinders on what then appeared to be a small dirty rabbit. We followed his grubby footprints all the way to Sweden, where Grandma Nordstrom was trying to light an ancient cannon that was now only a statue.

ALL YOUR BABY VOLCANOES

The shape has a clay—

it is me! So small, very

small, so I have been bent

in the earth and made red and sleepy.

Stay awhile, John. The mystics

are behind your eyes. Close the candle.

Lift the teeny hands.

Nobody knew then what fruit could do.

Don't smoke me so fast out of my stump.

One of those cunning extras.

THE WORD REVEALED OUT OF DARKNESS WAS   PEAR

someone has been writing
on your perfect menu

and your spirit has left you
for a stranger passing by your home

in the basement
i brew tea
and a list of rebuttals

a shadow hums in my window
as dusk la-tee-das
behind the mountain

the fruit was bold
to appear that way

and no one prepared
for the smaller wars

A LITTLE BLACK HOUSE ON THE SEASHORE

Sometimes, in the nice world, you fight over who is more sorry. No one gets prizes, but everyone's consoled. The more I think, the less there is to complain about and people get real shiny. A fire ripped across the prairie the day I was born and the darkness that followed was beautiful; the wheat reemerging, pure gold against the cinders. Our tiny hearts bowed down within us, and they did.

CARRY ON, NINEVAH

Let me speak to you now, from the fish's belly

with weeds around my head.

It's about preaching the right preaching:

pity the child, and also much cattle.

The earth is full, to and fro.

I say, bounding into the sky.

Spring up, waterfall!

But you must remain different.

How, matched with strength,

you down a bowl of raisins,

a herd of ponies outside your window.

The flight, the clean grey suit of it,

dabs at tracing away,

the perishing merely apparent.

Your newly arms

averted, carry on.

(A PRECARIOUS LIFE) ON THE SEA

the ocean you grew up watching has decided, finally, to take you in. "where else was i going to go?" you ask, setting off. it spews squid and minnows into your little boat for you to eat if you are hungry. you throw them back because you know the ocean is hungrier. at night, the moon casts a sidelong glance into your boat. you are less round. the ocean is delighted with your company. it carries you from place to place, each day a little easier, imagining your bright bones, sideways moons, it'll use them as walking sticks.

FOR I BELIEVED IN THE EXISTENCE OF WAITING
FOR LAUNDRY

4.

see this alone i found
god made human beings straightforward
but they searched for many complications

5.

i did learn one thing
we were completely honest when god created us
but now we have twisted minds

6.

see this alone I have found
that god made man upright   and they—
they have sought out many devices

'FESSIN FOR THE MONARCH

A thousand suitors came to tell the undersea rock garden they were truly sorry. The waves that made the garden were giants with helpless feelings. A rock will only grow up the way you shape it to, like monogamy, they explained. "Gee, I'm living in the world," said a suitor.

I love you, I confessed to a butterfly. May I lecture you? The sky pelted us with glories. "You should get some," the butterfly declared. "Cravings should be a big deal." I agreed but lost my hat in the drifting of the continents.

Take me to a medieval city so we can be reborn. It's been long nights imagining you in the usual skin, smoked out of your latest hiding place. I will, as they say, drink up my worries. Make good the evil bits. Yes, I would have written, but no, I didn't have the money. XO.

AT LEAST BEST, IT DIDN'T MATTER

Drunk on a postcard of an almond tree, eyeing the rings of figs made around the photo of the plumb line. A basket of summer fruit swilling flowers. The solid gold lampstand flung with underwear. And the seven lamps made of slung light, making seven channels through the bedsheets. The happy thought of being not in one's own sweater, watching the boiling kettle tilt north beside the fixed coffee maker and the flying love scroll of the done dishes. Coming across the poem in an old book. Smell of eggs and shallots, the up-earthing phantom.

HIS DEATH LEFT NO CAPITAL OF THE WORLD, NEITHER HERE NOR ANYWHERE ELSE

let us sail to greener waters

so we leave the rosebush behind
for the aphids to invent lace

when we set out
old leaves fall from the hull

see   even the sea
has cloaked itself
in ash

BLESS THE MIDDLEFRUITS

This is the Lord the day has made.

I will satisfy to be like being awake.

The enemy still hangs out in the cupboards

(the hands grow cold, from time to time).

My head on my own sword. Refrain.

Lord, don't you dam your streams

of loving-kindness. Rejoice more.

Let me be the marking seal,

the gardener deposit.

The bicycle was markedly whimsical, sporting features such as a weave of fake plastic flowers in its basket and a coat of rosy spray paint. Another key point is that perhaps the sinister looks of myself and my twin, especially in our bedraggled patchy coats and with our greasy mongrel hair, were an indication to the passerby that the bicycle was, for example, stolen, though the first thing to remember is that my twin was merely holding the bicycle, specifically so that our sister could don her mitts, and that she in her bold pink helmet, which stood out because of its deviation from the ordinary (as if determined, for instance, by caprice), should have been the most compelling evidence to indicate that the bicycle did belong to her and was not, in fact, "hot." On nights such as these in the city of Montréal, especially on the west end of Sainte-Catherine heading east, it is surprisingly difficult to avoid unsound townsfolk and, frankly, there are frequently more unsound than sound townsfolk on any given night. With this in mind, on the positive side, the whole situation was "pas grave."

ON YOUR BROKEN EVENING OF WET LEAVES

when the door opens and closes
i begin to understand rhythm

as indisputable as the night
bright with someone else's stars

where will you go now that you've finished with the farm?

in my dreams   your horizon
does not emerge

in my dreams   i am against you
and your streams

what end? you say

the keys and the door are still there
in the morning

STORY OF A LEAF

CHAPTER 1

I leaf. I come to my means. I tip the branch—a final hymn note. I am the feast. The sun-spent afterthought, wasted west. A basement of light. The same letter of an alphabet. The foreign wind chant. The summer's amnesia. The numb sum of it. The sieve of last light. The tree's last count. The damned sweetener.

BIPPITY

John woke up late and heart-crutchy to the world. The smell of
no-toast tumbled down into his rickety soul. His hip was sore from
having slept on a conch all night, but he did not wake up beside
the sea. Arrives a time when you awake to find your fuck-storm
apartment isn't the semicircular apse you once thought it was, John
thought in the dark and still. It was early. He couldn't hear or see
well. Just his bent-fork luck. Bars in Chicago could suck your mind
dry of homespun-apron-cherry-pie thoughts for a time—or times—
if you were lucky. Don't push it, he said to no one. You make too
much demands. He went to the patio and had four five six seven
cigarettes. The numb terracotta ash planter mustered dust. A dozen
or so smaller birds landed on the trees to shake off a few more
leaves. Look at what you've done, they clucked. This begs thought,
said John, who turned a heel towards the fridge and the indoors. On
the couch, the beer in his glass got smaller and smaller. He knew
his bones had seashell-shaped incisions where beds of roses used
to be. There was a liturgical element to his "these days" but without
the holy bit. The air rang. Oskar groaned over the telephone, and
decided not to come over that day—or anymore—having been a
radical who's travelled overseas, not some holed-up dump sluggard
on a couch with a small beer that's smaller-getting. When John
closed his eyes he was in a kindly field, green and ashless, where the
song of a large mammal spun itself into the lanks of earthly wind
that surrounded his head like a rosy mind-fortress or rogue kite.
Here, I will be loved, he thought. I can feel it just. The rosebush
he neglected returned as a no-longer-yellow vixen and combed her
thorns through his shabby hair as forgiveness. This is what I'll be,
he thought, from now on, a forgiveness-getter. The world broke into

a smile and ten thousand and one daisies anointed his brand-new thought. It wasn't any more interesting than that. He slouched off the tent of his reverie, which was starting to leak, and moved towards the weeping fridge to get another drink to quickly disappear. Took to the bathroom and saw the lard-tangle of his left hair. It always ends like this, he thought, putting down the beer and dumping baby powder into his mop. You can smell the baby but the baby might never be there. A fine coating of powder had landed on his shoulders. He felt like pudding. A single-battered deep-fried chip-shop black pudding, sliced open. Maybe he would move. Maybe he would become a hieromonk or a hegumen or an archangel. But first, he would caulk the counter where the dish rack had been and the water dribbled through. These are the only rehearsable mysteries. There are worse men, he thought at his reflection, and made his way back to the kitchen through a forest of bottles. In his mind, his home was catless because no cat ever trusted him. Who's to say it'd be any different. The honey of his summers had melted years ago, leaving the comb. No prospects for the future. For friends, maybe a few mindless votes. For family, a failed meeting of the minds.

TWIN FLAME

At the funeral home: a hum
of bread in the mouth,
a wine spark and some holiness
in the form of Brussels sprouts.

O Lord, I am consoled.
I am a rabbit in a field of easters.
I am with my bread and my oil.
I am not in need.

My friends salute me
from beyond the grave.
Who would have thought—
the finest bread, the finest oil?

WITH A FLICK OF THE WRIST I FASHIONED AN INVISIBLE ROPE, AND CLIMBED IT AND IT HELD ME

I came aboard a plane as one about to embark on a snowbird migration. I came above a cloud-plain, across a desire to enter it—to go after the blurred blue—against my better judgment, along a flight path, I came a long way. I entered alongside other snowbirds stuffed in large cars amid broad roads, among broad buildings. I came anti-establishment. It was around Christmastime. I came as an estuary.

FOR I BELIEVED IN THE EXISTENCE OF MORNING DRINKS

7.

see i have found only this
that god made men right
but they have found many sinful ways

8.

there is no other thing I have learned
god made people good
but they have found many ways to be bad

9.

but i did find this
god created people to be virtuous
but they have each turned to follow
their own downward path

I WANT TO KNOW WHERE THE HOUSE OF AN INSTANT OF SEEING IS

it was too hot to wear your sweater
but you'd already begun leaving

paused in a ring of hushed cows
a pasture past the shallow stream

what were you thinking?

it was always the hardest thing to imagine
not being eternal

The act of disembarking on the streets of Montréal, especially Sainte-Catherine, can be unpredictable and, all things considered, in the final analysis, in case of a disaster[1] or merely a stroll, as shown above, anything can happen, even bewildering conversations, and in the long run, it may be better to deny the peripatetic impulse and stay inside since (a) a sudden event, such as an accident or natural catastrophe that causes great damage or loss of life and other such unfortunate consequences, could strike at any moment and in any magnitude perhaps (b) involving one or multiple disasters and (c) these could occur with such abruptness and surprise that (d) walking would become unnecessary or (e) useless. Given these points, (f) walking, as it has been noted, and (g) the reasons to learn it (given that one does not have a dog), could (h) in a word be (i) "futile," but for the most part, (j) walking (especially with a twin) had become, (k) after all things considered, (l) quite enjoyable and, in fact, (m) to learn to walk long distances at a time (in a go), (n) in summary, was (o) not only important to (p) train oneself to survive certain disasters, (q) to improve one's health and (r) also conducive to writing something notable, but (s) enjoyable. In conclusion: (t–z) these considerations alone were enough to outweigh the possibilities of risk, discomfort, and such.

---

1. ...including but not limited to floods, volcanic eruptions, earthquakes, tsunamis, avalanches, limnic eruptions, landslides, hurricanes, cyclones, mud flows, ash clouds, blizzards, drought, wildfires, hailstorms, lava flows, heat waves, tornadoes, lightning, bush fires, epidemics, flus, SARS, AIDS, H1N1, XDR TB, malaria, solar flares, gamma-ray bursts, ice slides, famines, plagues, tuberculosis, typhoons, and torrential rains.

CHAPTER 2

I am teething with beams. I am likening. I am kinding from the boughs. I am minding the stem. I am lisping yellow across a coast of green. I am keeping notes on the smallest animals. I am blessing the gnarled reaches. I am filling with sea dreams. I am dancing stomatas. I am nooning my election.

EST. _____

Oh, I am well-fed. A grape

at the tip of the grapevine.

Frame me, hang me.

Oh, a pretty picture be.

The blade is off the plate, John.

The Yankees are waltzing again

and, everywhere, taste grows. The journey

sounded good to the deflowered.

Is it a glove or a mitt this time?

The egg's boiled stiff.

The crust's abandoned again,

the body.

Astride two years, at midnight, atop a concert hall in the deep south,
according to custom but maybe a bit ahead of time, a kiss à la italiana,
along with a request to dance, apart from everyone of course, but as for
me, aside from a desire to join the other waltzers, as per tradition, as to the
question, well I might as well as saying no have backed away.

As a result, since the sun had suddenly rebegun to shine (despite having little to no effect on the temperature, which remained, dismayingly, cold), and even in proximity to the upcoming calamity, being sunny and still predisaster, the day was perfect to set out on the Longest Walk and, under these circumstances, I phoned my twin, who agreed to meet me on Rue Saint-Denis between Rue Cherrier and Avenue Laurier and we donned our sunglasses and winter coats and for this reason completely missed one another and henceforth decided not to wear sunglasses at the same time. Thus the planned portion of the walk was postponed and, because la journée was not quite young, the Longest Walk became shorter, though indeed we had been travelling at a regular, slow pace by lifting and setting down each foot in turn the whole time, stopping and turning, then backtracking, until we found each other, but certainly the proposed route and our embarking upon it was delayed. Hence, once we'd found each other, the Longest Walk began, for we decided to ascend the mountain as, consequently, so did many others (including four horses and more than four dogs), and therefore the climb (which could hardly be called a climb though the lingering ice did make it difficult) to which we thereupon turned was commenced forthwith, and we turned accordingly off Rue Saint-Denis, down Avenue du Mont-Royal towards Parc du Mont-Royal.

COMB YOUR HORSES

You have filled your holy backpack

with ripe fruit and are bruised

from experimental dancing.

A kiss on the cheek!

One, two, three, four

and again John is on the floor.

The cheese stays sharp. The dog

agog with cotton possibilities.

And when we receive our handfuls

of holy walnuts, you will come too

coming to.

Everyone came bar Gershwin, and barring a miracle, I was the youngest there. Before the band stopped playing, behind a curtain, below some gaudy chandeliers, beneath the plastic noise of noisemakers, beside a dropped flute, besides it being the appropriate occasion, wedged between waltzers, beyond six glasses of champagne but still "by Jove" awake enough to dance because of Gershwin, but for your sake, by means of a snack bar, I stalled.

CHAPTER 3

I fell. I tufted a clamorous spirit. I took care. I wrote my name in classical Japanese. I turned as I went. I turned as a boat on the waves. I harmed nothing. I bore my death's descent. I jayed the light that sank in everywhere. I read no maps. I doused the air. I passed beyond meekness. I fainted in the liquor of autumn. So I went.

BOPPITY

Two women siphoned by. John let an awkward smile, down-looking,
not seeing if it was returned. He was on the streets of Chicago.
The streets were all over him, teasing his soberness. Get offa me,
he said. A newborn passerby frowned, hustled on past the food
stands. John loved fast-moving pencil skirts. He followed the pencil
skirt for a bit, out of boredom. He wasn't looking for the nearest
bar, because he knew where they all were. None of them had pencil
skirts. No pencil skirts with soft pretzely asses underneath. No
cherry lipstick or homemade painstake curls. Just sinewy blondes
with cheez whiz smiles and Tennessee tees and Forty Creek. No,
those women won't do. The unwholesome need the wholesome.
John was looking for a gingham saviour. A messianic pencil skirt.
He wasn't about to give up, because he'd already given up years ago.
It was his forty-third birthday. Which was his best? he wondered.
The one when all of heaven had sent its angel-hoard alighting on his
dark soul? But no point in thinking of the younger years. I am here,
and here, he thought, not there. Unfeeling the best. Uncourteous,
in private. The night before, he'd dreamt he'd slowly sheared off his
hands, right below the fingers. A glance to a lookatwhatyou'vedone,
John. Unforgiveness. Old fodder. Hand rot and sad sad sad. No
chance this was not a dream, he thought. And then his fingers grew
spritefully back. Small and nubbinly. Oh, when will this night be
over? Vouchsafe me, pencil skirt. John was self-declared too unprim
anyways. Sensitive about an aversion to fish. Unweddable. Acres
of aversion, every day. Everybody everywhere putting God away
except for John, wracked with the birdshadow of the spirit, glade of
guilt gliding over him, pecking at his ne'er-do-well tendencies. John
resolved to never drink again, and thought he could last maybe an
hour. Stepped into a nearby chattery café. The ladies were all well-
set in the café. John knew if he were to ever wake again, it would
be in the slender soapy arms of a woman with her fingers linked
round a mug hook. Coaxing it upward to her peripheral lips. Her

wifey birthday lips. The air was flung with talk that would not stop.
Sweet milky ships of amicability. This is beautiful: a tumble in the
valiant sober café, teeming with three thousand perfect statues of
the public, lips pursed and spreading, a walled garden of laughter,
unshitfaced. John did not want a coffee. He drifted, painfully
mannered, composing his hands in memory of his dream. This
was not his place, it was theirs. The unfilled air is crying, Get out of
here. Twist in the corridors of feeling for no one but yourself. John
moved through the empty café space, twisting his hands like jar tops
coming off and going on. He was dancing down the chimneys of his
rotting soul. He could not swim back. He was ill. A grocery list of
winters. His head bent low, all in backward moments. The shocking
touch of his head, with the blood all in it, on the nervous café floor.
John's dead head, the corresponding O, the luck, uncoming.

ASHES OF INCONCEIVABLE ARTS

when you broke a plate on the radiator
i knew it was time

somewhere a man
is wearing a belt of pure gold
standing in astroturf
surrounded by dragonflies
he can't see i said

the dragonflies are setting their cruciforms
in his hair
he's trying to tell you something

listen   he's saying

who hasn't compared the night
to an alley?

HAPPY BIRTHDAY, IN A NICE WAY

One last flame, fork face-down.

Sprinkles bleeding in the cream.

We stayed friends. Writing

every two or three months.

All those years.

Better be good for the next ones.

Drink our glasses of holy blood.

The patterns in the upholstery moved

around us like a forest under a godly wind.

And when you come home

take the black lab back

to the mud lake

and weep for me there, John,

by the mud lake.

Circa 2012, concerning snow, considering the lack thereof and counting on it contrary to popular opinion and despite the impossibility of it coming down during a December evening in Florida in a gallery-cum-concert hall close to the ocean, I came outside to observe. Because depending on the state of the climate due to rumours of global warming, snow would not be possible tonight and, except in extraordinary circumstances, would never happen, excepting that one incident on January 19th in 1977 when, excluding those who slept through the brief and early hour of snowfall, Floridians young and old (except for the too young and the too old), following each other to their front porches, came to gaze, for the first time, at the fragile powder landing on the bewildered palms.

I AM NO MORE THAN A SECRETARY OF THE INVISIBLE THING

the world is sometimes with us
and it is

green blades fawning
round your beautiful white boots

presence makes what?
absence
absence

CHAPTER 4

I was eye-longing. I was rendering seasons. I wasn't stopping. I was billing winter. I was birding blindly. I was churning the memory of my flight. I was glooming the jump. I was housing summer months between me. I was self-imagining. I was furnishing grey. I was thinning bedless sleep. I was shallowing the heights. I was reciting the moss, the wintry pity.

I AM ONLY AN ONLY CHILD

Lord, you are the Observer.

All we wanted was someone

to teach everybody something.

Keep a record.

I am only an only child. I don't know

how to come or go.

My soul waits for your soul,

flipping stones.

Cradle me, Lord, as someone

who still loves the dead.

And king me through the hedges

when I go.

An hour later, although we were for the most part absorbed in conversation as we passed the walkers, joggers, runners, idlers, horseback riders, and cross-country skiers, along with their animals if they had them, we spotted a dog who, instead of walking as normal dogs do, galloped like a pony. I declared that this must be because it is "si heureux," and hardly had the words exited my mouth than my twin responded that, in fact, it could be that the dog was injured, which then would render him "not a happy dog." "How cruel," I exclaimed, "for its owner to gallop it up the mountain if it is injured, in case that its injury worsen or even bother it." "Yes," my twin replied, "but there are many sad dogs." This was said in order that I might gain some perspective, and truly to be sad for the sake of this small dog seemed unproductive, though indeed, at the time, it made me feel worse to ponder all the dogs that were somewhere unfortunately and regrettably characterized by sorrow and regret. "To put it differently," my twin said, "provided that this one dog causes so much grief in you, is it not only fair to think of all the other dogs who might be injured or somehow sorrowful and therefore alleviate your singular sadness?" I replied, "Now that this one has come to my attention, I find it does more good to sympathize with the single sad dog, once seen, rather than exhaust or dilute one's emotions thinking of all the other sad dogs that may or may not exist on this planet. Besides, there is still a possibility that this sad dog ahead of us might be a happy dog." "Rather than argue," my twin said, "since we always come to the same conclusions, why don't we ascend to the Kondiaronk Belvedere? I brought apples since I knew you would be hungry."

I AM THE STAMPEDER

Surely, you also desire

the burn that turns

the glass black.

You no longer delight in dead animals

or I would bring some.

Here's a shabby bull heart

to prove me right.

From inside the hall's courtyard, just forward of it, I saw a wild mangrove and figured I would move further towards it, given that they were famous and that I'd come all this way, having gone south in a plane (including a stopover in New York, in addition to a predicted missed flight between that city and Fort Myers in case of a storm and then in face of a storm, in favour of safety in front of said storm, in lieu of landing on time, in spite of the inconvenience, instead of taking a risk in view of the circumstances, because it was less than three hours to the next flight to Fort Lauderdale though it is not so near to Fort Myers, notwithstanding my new arrival time being 1:00 a.m.), due to the hassle of my getting to this particular place, I felt compelled to enter the mangrove.

BOO

Mid-afternoon. John on the café floor. Splayed corpse pose. Passed out or dead. Mind-phantoms, like fruit flies, on his dead peach heart. Narrator's voice in his head. Everything in his head. John, sometimes-speaking. If there are other characters, other sounds, John is unaware of them. Hands clenching. Ambiguity. No curtain.

NARRATOR (OR SOMETIMES JOHN): John...Yohanan...Ioannes... time he backwards went...come bury me, now and then...the drowsy evil floating on the afterscene...no good, this John... all elbow bones...a dirt-person...uninterrèd...the world's leavinghimsolo...told you he was long self-slain...if so: coming unshrinely...so sick of the litter...uneasy dolly under the public's constant everywhere-glancing...so low...for John is a stenchful future-bruiser...and so is John all!...brimming shoulder-high rot-thoughts...comes John to speak at his own depth-side...John is his frenemy, blighted in the womb, possibly shrineful...but the excellencies say John is stenchful... and John brought his soiled shoulders to an unspeakable peace...whose ransoms dribbled four unbearable decades and three dumb years...did this seem stenchful?...when others glanced, John crawled with his ghosts...stenchfulness should be a holier wonder: flighty sabbath girls...yet the world says it be stenchfulness...and the holy brain is by then disappeared... upon the bed frame's sinewy hand, John no babies begat, his ladies grimly married off...was this stenchfulness?...yet John says I am stenchful...and sure I am a mind-battering man... but here I speak to what I am justly knowing...I did love myself once, without function...o judgment, let me not open your letters on my writing table...I have lost my uplooking face...after so long, at last...do not think so, John...you shall not find your plans so lately sunburnt...the neck-wrapping radio cords...and God forgive the dazed carnivores of the graduating world who've shut your phantom-swarming soul out in the lisping night...no one to redeem John's worldwide head...and, in the fermenting of John's lingering day, be bold to tell the night-ladies he is the hundred latest plates on their laps...when will he wear a smooth nape of blood?...and furnish his miskismets with glistering champion costumes... which, stripped away, shall jostle John's glooms deep in his hobo coat...the lightlack...John, get up, child of export ale and female tennis matches...bellowing reptilic John, cigarette-phlegm knight...your unthought-of mental pain...enough shared...every official verdict dead...would they were a field of choiring shepherds staring at a light on your head...shames, undoubled...for once...no time to switch gnashing deeds for fondness-spasms...praying his half-contempt...good lord...his gross deeds to their ends...John, called by his fizzling wrongs to such greasy graves...chancing every inbuilt beauty...the slightest neighbour's wife...to tout each gutter of his heart... this in the God-name...the frozen water which pleaseth he...I shall sentiment, o lord...do...please salve...the long-lashed wounds of incompetence...the cancelling ends...the hundred billion lacks...the smallest

IT LOOKED NICE FROM THE TOP OF THE JOURNEY

O God, I will be satisfied to

sit in the pews of the wheat chaff.

I wait at the tip of your whisker.

Give me this day. And that one too.

Spent hours teaching the weather to stop.

You loved, you bared your best foot.

Your spirit shuffles down the fields

and I drop a coin into its just-was.

Lord, might you find me there soon.

Atop some moving mountain,

threshing a new flame,

looking upwards,

your soul-forfeiter not.

Into the stilt-root jungle, cautious like an egret, minus the sure-footing, next to the Gulf of Mexico, near the heart of Vanderbilt Beach, I went off the trodden path, on my own, onto the cypress knees; opposite the strangler figs, outside the brackish water, over the reindeer lichen, on account of a feeling of angst on behalf of having come too far on board a plane, on to this new terrain, on top of a root knot grown opposite to my understanding of root growth other than the poison ivy which grew in my yard in Canada, which I discovered also happens to be an aerial root (and, in fact, is not really ivy) by means of an abandoned encyclopedia outside of a house that was destroyed owing to a hurricane.

IT WAS NOT IN PARKS THAT I LEARNED HUMILITY

despite doom's declarations the grass
continues to grow

self-pity may be another form
of selfishness

but could you please play your accordion elsewhere?

to make up for your loss
i become you

the dust in certain ancient
unfound caves
is as unimaginable
as the black bones it hides

call for sulphur
and a flood   and the wind
breaks the pond

no   do not call the animals
or send a dove

do not send a raven
or sink to that mountain

NOBODY COMING

At the top of her journey, Johanna cracked a lager. She was thirteen
and thinking of the beautiful, smothering western sea. The concrete
stoop leading down to it from her old house, in the coastal town
where she used to live. Don't let me be lonely, she said to her
memory. After all, I am nobody coming. She hummed a little to
stave off the sadness then took a step towards away-from-home. The
beer made her mouth dry and sour-tasting. Damn beer, she thought,
but didn't mean it. The lager was somebody else's, anyways. In the
outdoors, the winter brewed its long and dark. Above Johanna, the
stars handed out wonderment, but didn't share. She heard beasts in
the sidelong woods, and pictured black fangs and mermaid tails, long
talons and Kraken masks. She wasn't scared, though. She pretended
they protected her from something that looked like the absence
of them. It might just be best to leave me behind me, Johanna
considered. She was known for holding herself back from things,
and nothing very bad had happened to her lately. Life can be a doily
in your grandmother's home, if you let it be, she believed. If you're
lucky, you'll be pretty, but unanimous, with a prettier thing either
above or below you to soak up all the attention. She harboured with
her the type of sadness that comes from looking too long at a lake
or a mountain. But she didn't feel sad here, on a road through the
woods full of monster-protectors and ogling stars. Each step of her
small boots sent echoes of power against everything she was blind
to. She thought of her grandmother, back at home, conked under
layers of Swedish blankets. Johanna would be back before morning.
An hour passed and she reached the mud lake. It looked beautiful
from afar, like a regular lake. Johanna had discovered it was the
only body of water in this small, dried-up town. It was dark, and still
nobody was coming, so Johanna went down to the water's edge. It
was lined with stones. She pulled a can of paint from her pack, and
a wide brush, and started painting each rock belly-white. She was an
eighth of the way around the small lake when it turned time to stop.

Light rose like steam off the pines and her grandmother would be awake within the hour. Nobody watched her scratch the paint off her palms in the mud lake, hammer the lid back on the can, and draw her small body up from the water's edge to the dewy road bound for home. She didn't hear the beasts this time and the stars had all but perished. Life in the light is boring, she said. No one heard her. Her heart was full of the valley. When she upped the stoop, she saw that her grandmother's shoulders were cloaked pink and hunched at the table over a bowl of mush. She didn't ask Johanna where she had been. She didn't turn to face her. She said the wolves had come last night, howling as though the moon had multiplied, right above their very own home, which was also everybody's home, which was what it meant to be welcoming. She said their song was slow and infinite, the way bones feel. The old lady moved towards the window. Johanna's heart was busy with silence. She looked up to where the moons were fading. "Oh come on down. Oh come on down," said her grandmother, as Johanna went up the stairs to sleep.

PERHAPS THE MUSEUM NEVER EXISTED

Maybe everything is good, after all.

The act of reading and the act of understanding

made it. The point is, relates to reality.

No wonder.

And what of this?

Precise laws. Behaviour of individuals.

Unintentional walk. Maps of maps.

Wheels on the table legs. The main activity

continuous drifting, these visions.

Dear professional juxtaposer,

maintain a division.

Cyberspace, I walked across it.

I'm a little disappointed.

Where the body is, at the corner.

Past the roseate spoonbills pending flight, one step per minute (plus a couple more), learning pro-creeping preparatory to my sudden panicked realization of alligators, prior to a more logical thought re: fear regarding the danger of alligators and the simple act of respecting their space, thinking of the rough beasts floating round the swamp regardless of my presence (and perhaps now due to my presence), save for the immersed and saving those that were sleeping, since they were nonetheless imminent (at least psychologically), save for that tree I at once climbed, I would surely have perished.

THINKING MYSELF IMPORTANT BY CANDLELIGHT

how will i answer
the smaller flame
its crooked wick

i spend mercy
on whites and reds

can't look
past the glass

though i sometimes
set out the saucer

for the shapes of clouds
on certain nights

NOT AS ASCENSION.

Torn up in the surgery of night. The buttering under of it. Seven halos away from becoming a sprig of something anointed. Never too few in the brooding door frames; the spoken-to lighting the walls. The corner-drawing minds buttoning silver horns of ancient wisdom. A voice: Dance with me, future loser, I love you. Hide under the table, I will call down the Lord without sulphur. To cast alms over our future mistakes.

PROPHECIES OF MY YOUTH FULFILLED BUT NOT IN THE WAY ONE EXPECTED

a beast arrives in radiant colours
to walk among us

the looks were stern
from many sheep pens

you would be happy to know
the garden has been maintained

and either i always meant to leave
or never did

turn the sheep away
and i'll spend my life as a bear

again undone
and so full of shit

FOR I BELIEVED IN THE EXISTENCE OF UNDERCONFIDENCE

10.

lo this only have i found
that god hath made man upright
but they have sought out many inventions

11.

behold this is the only [reason for it that] i have found
god made man upright   but they [men and women]
have sought out many devices [for evil]

12.

i have found only this
god made people decent
but they look for many ways
[to avoid being decent]

NOT AS ASCENSION.

It has driven you mad. The left towns. The river. The twisted ankles of the chosen ones, stunting across your vision. Desirous to be atop any building, moving moon-dumb into someone else's night. You are alone. But it has become the community feeling. Take a harmonica when you go. Bid adieu to the feeling of it. The gold ring of living in it.

IN VALLEYS OF BEAUTIFUL, THOUGH POISONED, RIVERS

eyes closed i saw violas   yellow road lines
the bellies of salmon

the single window
of your childhood bedroom
choked in insulation

you said the pines had raised their combs
against you   a thousand
cocked silver eyes

NOT AS ASCENSION.

A confession to take me to the burrow—the gracious stump—the holy furrow where we can lose our legs for a while, off a green coast. The silt road's souring in my wake. My coming to. Left to bend suns across it: harden the fall. I'm sorry, watchdogs of my youth, for letting go so. And to the new and coming: I'm sorry. Never meant to fold so. Pull over, glory. What is your name? Let me be the blimp that carries it way way up.

PSALM OF AFTER-YEARS

Clutched in the frame

of ninety tries, hinge-broke

at you. No known testimonial.

Maybe I will come to your palace of glory.

Maybe you will answer me there.

Stopped in its threshold,

throwing the static of the blown fire.

Oh gardener of the last light.

Oh sky-sun, burned dumbly out.

NOT AS ASCENSION.

Sitting, watching the disease spread over. Incurring the register of
the who, who passed mid-nightly. Have your talk with me, stranger,
then turn to. Let me soak it off. But remind me of the beauty of the
tall tall grass. The tall tall grass. The liquid sway. The golden united
tongues. The long choir. My skin thin to its surface: move under it,
like a million feet of what's been done, taking every path.

HELLO. DEAR.

Hello, dear. Remember the great flood? The one where, when the
water started, everyone donned colourful swim caps and nabbed
whatever floating milk cartons they could find and splashed around
in joy and wonder wishing their children's children and parents'
parents could have experienced what it is like to swim in one great
lake with all your friends and future and past friends like a big
enamoured family on an eternal summer vacation with everyone
in their bathing suits but happy anyway and thinking of ways we
could all work together to build a raft or floating bouncy palaces with
attached trampolines so we could bounce from one castle to another
on days we didn't want to get wet which would be no days because
who doesn't want to always be swimming in a great lake with all your
friends when the water's rising and lifting you higher and higher
towards the place we have always wanted to explore—that is, the
sky—whether we admit it out loud or in our dreams or not; granted,
we were all now lucky to be flying into a dream of giving the world a
big bath, ducks and all. All of this to say, I hope you are well and have
started thinking positive thoughts because you know it was positivity
that made everyone buy colourful swim caps in the first place and
accomplish their dreams of building castles in the sky—dreams
made possible only by being carried there by rising waters which,
on anybody else's terms, would have been terrifying and certainly
tragic but, as you can see, everyone was prepared by the unanimous
decision to throw a party no matter where or with whom since life
is "futile" without celebrating every turn, whether up or down; it is
these natural happenings to which we must turn when forced to
consider what it means to be a human being floating in this world,
and not lament the colour of swim cap you chose or how it divided
you into teams or why the purple team stole the canvas straight
from the top of your trampoline, which was petty and irksome but,
in the great ocean of things, doesn't matter in the teeniest—what
really does is that we have all floated up to this together in the Great

World Bath and we should focus on finding half-full bottles of soap in the surface debris to empty into the waters to enhance the cleanliness and softness of our new world beneath us and try not to clash soap flavours but rather make them harmonious like the smells of a baby forest or cake shop which we may never see again but can get close to by dumping out pine and musk soaps or vanilla and cinnamon but not all four at once, oh no, dear, that would not do at all. All this to say, even in great flooding and powerful parties we must not forget the delicate noses of the people. All the very best.

So that we would cease in our argument, I conceded to ascend to the Kondiaronk Belvedere. The belvedere was higher than we imagined and by the time we reached the top, I was feeling sufficiently sore. Though walking had long been a pastime of mine, the nagging pain I now experienced on the Kondiaronk Belvedere caused me to question the sense of walking in a city, especially up a hill, or worse, down a hill, with the knowledge that such walks would cause me pain. A part of me was tempted to consider this question, whereas my other part (to whom I listened more frequently) knew it is important to walk, whether in pain or no, to avoid the certain disaster, which, it is argued, is inevitable. Head aloft, I considered such complex things until a free-range child, who bounded vigorously into view, jumped upon a loose cement tile in front of me and lost balance, falling and scraping his left side. This happened despite there being several orange cones, the reason for whose presence was ambiguous, which is why, in my opinion, the child is owed compensation from whoever is responsible for the looseness of those thin slabs of concrete (supposedly shaped according to the purpose for which they were required) and the unsatisfactory placement of several orange cones.

FOR I BELIEVED IN THE EXISTENCE OF
SEVENTY-TIMES-SEVENS

13.

only this i have found
that god made man right
and he hath entangled himself
with an infinity of questions

14.

one thing i have learned [found]
god made people good [virtuous upright]
but they have found all kinds of ways
to be bad [sought out many devices]

15.

i found this only
that god made a man rightful
[that god made man right]
and (then) he meddled himself
with questions without number

16.

(i found only this
that god made a person upright
or clear-headed
but then he mixed himself in/mixed himself up
with too many questions)

CHAPTER 5

I have come to my end. I have dressed in superb costumes. I have spent my last days without. I have prowled the reaches of sleep. I have scribbled your breath as thought. I have kept along. I have settled a home in the grass. I have wound the songs of light. I have connected parent and child. I have roosted among talons. I have appeared suddenly lost.

IF I AM SICK, THERE IS NO PROOF WHATSOEVER THAT MAN IS A HEALTHY CREATURE

the voice dies with the body
i cannot distinguish the meaning of this

so i come to believe
you were never real
always too much
with your goings

but a hundred dragonflies landed in my hair today

no one will believe this

Although this may be true, the orange-cone incident did not fully detract from the matter whose truthfulness, in contrast, was ambiguous as it depended on the right judgment of the current emotional state of a small animal. Of course I am referring to the happy dog/sad dog philosophical impasse, but how to come back to such matters after a small and concrete disaster had just taken place before our very eyes? On the other hand, the tumble could give the discussion new force, as upon observing the rolling about on the ground of the child by the cones, one must ask oneself if one sympathizes with this particular child, all children who have ever fallen over loose tiles amid orange cones, or with all children who indeed are suffering and have suffered not just tumbles upon belvederes but far more grievous tribulations. At the same time, I had the inkling that in spite of this dog and this child and their consequent joy or sadness— whether imaginary or no—the real question ever so elaborately masked was whether or not one's habit, dare I say one's "désir," was to embody the sadness of the sad dog.

MY NEIGHBOUR'S MISFORTUNE PIERCES ME AND I BEGIN TO COMPREHEND

for a.t.

i too skipped the part
        about the grave clothes
                and saturday

and the bomb going off
        forever

what i couldn't see my whole life
        let me tell you now
                a lamp has several sides   aha

you have been found wanting
no one can stand your assemblies
        the deep says "you are not in me"
        and the sea says "you are not with me"

but one day everyone will help you
        peace will come   as always
                on the creaking wheels of some old fire

you've learned to not make idols of your bread
        to dwell in darkness
                        like a heart or lung

you will search
   though light bulbs will not bloom
    and flames creep on the vine
     the cassettes of the young knot
      and the fields yield many paths
       the flock is cut off from the fold
      and no sound followed
     our lack of reasons

SCARECROW COMMUNION

The outfits I wore beside the grave were not always black. Keep me from me, I ask you, but you don't hear and I don't expect you to. All the people come and kiss each other on the cheeks and you, my friend, beneath the ground, roll onto your right side. It takes a while to find more flowers to stuff into the old scarecrow. Cupped hands were always good for something. When I put the roses in its eyes, a voice: blessed are those who are sure of themselves, who take a fig, or don't.

CHAPTER 6

I have been kept along. I have been sober all my life. I have been a burning tongue in the fall. I have been winding up. I have been gunned gracefully by gusts. The moon has been moaning over me. I have been blazing into history. I have been unspeaking. I have been reading my life backwards. I have been indexing forgettable pages. I have been always coming to my end.

I DON'T UNDERSTAND HOW TO THINK
ABOUT THE DEAD

the valley's cracked palm
is unreadable   no road

just white stones circling mud
and the hills darkening to a low burn

somewhere coyotes
reckon over bone

take two steps
the earth is a blank stare
you enter alone

SHE WAS COLD, AWARE THAT SHE WAS NOWHERE

at the crossroads
take the good path
i will not walk in it

if i were to say go
be well fed and well
what use is it?

i forfeit my inheritance to the hound
chasing a white-tailed oracle
across the snow

it's a ghost's life
cutting flesh to the bone
dropping glass after glass
down the stairwell

SOMETHING PROPHECIES

What was it? Trying to remember what it wasn't you hadn't had enough of. I will go home. I will be well. Someone or other will call, and I will be glad not to answer.

All but the old faces will arrive. Sitting in spaces you didn't pay for. Keeping it. All you ever wanted, to take care of. Keep in mind.

CHAPTER 7

I had skulled the tip of summer. I had given the whole thing up. I had lined the tree's madness. I had gnashed to the end. I had had degrees of first flight. I had awarded myself nothing. I had limboed sullen selfhood and good order. I had waffled my brothers' names. I had left the tomb of increase. I had aged unseen water. I had interpreted private wonder.

PARTICULAR HEXES

White omens in the sky make shapes of us. I wear all my medallions at once. Found a snout in the basil plant. Who can blame. You, in the small frame. Glasses and long-suffering. I sent you a letter on the subject of broccoli. What's another word for sacrament?

Summer séances spent welcoming a new ice age in hospital gowns. No one visits, and if they do, we stick 'em. Wasn't coordinated enough to find a new castle. Always the first to go. No sons or daughters come to sing hymns around. Unmothered in the off-season.

A strange hand under a young chin. Most times, your dreamer is the enemy. I spend the night writing Westerns, answering yes and yes to true or false. I guess I need to live up to fatherhood. Grow my summer antlers. See how far the voodoo lily will stretch.

STORM FOR YOUR GOOD

Lord, may I harbour in the squalls
of your love. Send it over me—
leave a pink cloud. Let me call it
a dominion.

And when you take me back
to that inlet, I will try not to hear
any other voice. I will not
try to hear another voice.

THE ASTROLOGER SHOWDOWN

Looking up, I discovered I'd always been a young bore. The night sky made it always impossible to tell the difference between a river and a plain path. I move along it anyways, having dressed in fine denim, having been blest by the priest's son, then leered at by the bottom of the glass. I'm not used to having no one come when I call. The cupboard closes once more over my eyes, leaving a dusting of every day of my life on the carpet. Time to replace the rug. Beckon the new, but please don't.

WATCHING COYOTES PICK OFF THE CATS

i am ready to accept
invisible gifts   let me

drink mine
            and yours

what is it about this lamp
and exposure

where did i put my overflowing cup?

life has been easy
i am tipping your glass

to the feral dogs
and their mouthfuls of velvet

Be that as it may, I kept the question from my twin. Then again, I may have uttered something, since, above all, the conversation put its tail between its legs. But the mountain air was very nice. After all, we had come this far on an injury that I had thought nothing of fixing but for the prompting of my twin, indeed that I had not even noticed until we had breached the dangerous structure erected on the pleasure ground of Mont-Royal for the purpose of viewing the surrounding scene. Thus ended La Grande Promenade, with a descent down the south side of the mountain towards a small restaurant on Avenue Lincoln for Chinese dumplings. Still, days later, when the time came to see the medic, an action that contradicted my usual impulse to deny any such problems that may (and often do) at a later date prove detrimental, she told me that to walk or to run is henceforth forbidden (yet short distances are okay) as long as I, between appointments, perform various exercises to increase the strength of the conjunctions of certain bones that, albeit healthy, are weak and misused. "Besides," she said, "you took too long to see me."

Waiting in a tree being more than I could bear, I descended to inch back through the mangrove, throughout the hanging roots, till I came to the place touching moonlight where I was sure to find something noteworthy, towards the end of this expedition, towards a broken shaft in the overgrowth, thanks to some miracle of nature (together with its natural proceedings), under the branch-womb, underneath the clear sky, a shaft of light unlike any place I'd known, until a great blue heron up the tree, of whom up until that point I had been unaware, upon encountering the bird up against all odds (or at least having low odds up to the point when I decided to enter the mangrove), raised its wings versus the mangrove awning and took flight via the slim crack in the overgrowth, its clear grey body vis-à-vis the swamp-murk, with such ease and skill, within such a tangled maze, was without, which was worth celebrating, with reference to modes of escape and with regard to the difficulty of rendering them graceful.

Look ahead, John, there's a new coat of summer jackets and shoes without holes on the human planet. An hour stint, but already feeling bad for not seeing everyone is truly perfect. The waiter passes by your vision to never mind. I come around asking for change for a turnip and you give me some. When the pollen falls in our laps, I toast my great-aunt Blanche. She always thought I rode a horse, and I agreed so I rode it over the grass that coiled pathetically under the snow just in time for our worst Christmas ever. I remember it, but the name slips.

Although my pattern had been to focus on the greater and more foreboding disaster at hand, my attention instead, thanks to the hounding of my twin and the sound advice of a medic, had been brought to a tiny conjunction of bone on my lower right side. Whereas earlier I had been imagining the necessity of walking great distances for survival on streets as various and far between as the west end of Rue Sainte-Catherine and the north end of Rue Saint-Denis, despite myself, my very body had rendered the vision unimaginable until I conversely stopped my peripatetic practice and otherwise tended to the simple motion of lifting and lowering my right leg off the floor in one spot. However, her halting proclamation would not stop disaster from happening when it so chose, and rather than its timing being even slightly convenient, disaster struck nevertheless, regardless of my "insuffisance" and notwithstanding the above-outlined "road to recovery."

Keep me away from the garden, and I promise to have it out. Scratching wax off last night's table, you did feel bad. Expect advantageous changes this morning! Let yourself go and feel happy with the afternoon moon! The knife in your hand winks, but you aren't interested today. These confessions seem dull in the face of the widows among the orchids. Please remember, I was unfair because I loved you. When you ask, I'll tell you to give my books back to the trees and I'll hold those olive pits in my heart. Suck the salt, now and then.

THE WOBBLY SPLENDOUR OF THE SEA

friend   you will find your island   you will
dress as a monk and sing hymns
to invisible gods

do not look unkindly on yourself
you may not be granted passage

the pastures are already drying   the mountains
rubble   the world is a field of bones
that won't stand   a trumpet sounding
out of earshot

take to the place you long for
that grove of burnt trees
and distant lightning

leave us to argue
about who loved you best

FOR OVER TWO THOUSAND YEARS I HAVE BEEN TRYING TO UNDERSTAND WHAT IT WAS

I.

what was it again? deep snow?
in the end what was it?
a river?

another edge left me
wooing anything that soothed

i've been found wanting
you have

only so many oceans to cross
though we count them
in drops

CHAPTER 8

I had been glossing the skyline's throng. I had been going unnoted. I had been acting the monstrous beard of the tree. I had been stringing the drenched map of fate. I had been digging down in my stem. I had been cluttering the last thousand years. I had been raging stupendous and impure. I had been preserving the tree's rhymed hands. I had been flourishing among the great choiring bugs.

2.

a shoal of green reeds
always spelled escape
or sherry in the kitchen

where again the chairs are captive
to certain moods

again wonder
if i watered the dead
cactus too much or too little

THE BASKET WALTZ

It was around that time of year when everyone decides to take their chances. The baker transformed into a cut of meat, and the funeral was solemn, the casket oddly shaped. We hadn't learned any better, but then again, there was no one there to teach us. Asleep in the wild country, we watched the moths go up in flame.

Lay me down, prophets, and let me watch you read into things. It took only a couple of years to learn that the oracle is sometimes wrong. One day, I taught her how to French-braid her hair and from then on braids became powerful symbols of widows. She told her secrets only to the dog, and when she died, the dog ran off into the woods, taking our bones with him.

When my daughter returns as an old woman, she'll take up country singing. I'll take up lodging in a nearby tree next to several spiders. We'll spend our last days comparing webs, though I never will feel at the centre of mine. When my daughter passes, I'll spin each note of "Walkin' After Midnight" into perfect white skeins of yarn.

3.

at the party
one drink away
from something novel

you or an unborn child
appear somewhere as a rabbit
gone to the mountain
paws in the deep...

what was it? yes
sad   yes
should have skipped this

THE END, WHICH WAS THE BEGINNING

Cheers me, Lord. Set me alight

on the bowing field of friendship.

Hold me to the sun

and I will watch you from there—

hung in the light of your making.

Sing about horses in my nearness.

Sling me, beam-like, over summer's shoulder.

Catch its long story in my hair

and huddle with me on the balcony

of what I don't know.

Rest me

in some hands. All of them

reaching.

In the first place, the disaster was not only unexpected but it also happened on such a subliminal scale that, in fact, most everyone failed to notice it had occurred at all. For sure, disasters in like manner take place all over the map, in addition to all over other maps, and are coupled with comparable results: other folks, in the same way, are forced from their homes first from "l'insomnie," second from a desire to leave the disaster's aftermath, and third out of simply not knowing what else one could possibly do in the light of unsaid circumstances, not to mention all of this under a general blanket of lethargy. To say nothing of the others affected by similar disasters whose trauma is equally important, they, by the same token, were difficult to imagine—nearly impossible—by both myself and my twin who, again, advised me to fetch help, but the disaster having been so subliminal, to tell anyone who may be living in perfect happiness from lack of knowledge seemed unnecessary and again we set to walking—parkward towards Lafontaine.

A FLASH AND THE FABRIC OF THE WORLD IS UNDONE

on the sky the morning is red

are you sleeping? run
to the river
you're in love

look across the lit rooftops
an eye with the face of an eagle
a light in the abandoned house

the mosquitoes
back and forth
small drums of lightning

THANK YOU FOR THE BREAD RAIN

Lord, you are very great. You splendour

in tents and chariots on some upper waters.

At your garments, rebuke flees.

You lift the bowed-downers.

Your wine makes my face shine.

Give us your food with smells

of sacred biscuits.

Don't judge a shape by its apple, Lord.

I am letting them grow

for their shadows.

THE UNKEEPABLE PROMISES

I.

In a few minutes, I will exit the chariot that was a squash after all. The phone is dead. In a mysterious pocket of unhearing. It hasn't been daisies. Last night, I went out smoking. The Everly Brothers visited me in my sleep. You don't always have to give a damn. If I'm happy, my letters get bigger, like the outer leaves of a cabbage. The same, just bigger. Je vais attendre. Your hat was ridiculously tall. You were a soldier pretending to do something. Why do you always make me say it? There are twenty-nine sure places to set your feet on this earth and seventy-one unsure ones. That makes up the whole earth.

2.

Did you know your love is as many as the hairs on my head? The coyote moved back and forth, pondering the multitude. But the trees! Some cried and continued crying. Some people just look alike—it's that simple. It has nothing to do with spirits. I made a hammock for my heart out of a lemon rind and knew what it was. If only these things were as easy as couch patterns in the '60s. Time now is the hardest to put up with, even when time now is good and we are mourning time good's ending. The woman who enters sits too close and I cannot continue my conversation with myself, though it was getting good. Never take a break, crazy. Is it someone's birthday yet?

3.

Maybe your best friend has yet to be born, ever think of that? I spotted the glass with wary looks, waited to order another without sending back the first. This was always the trick of life. And good paper. I've been brushing my hairs for hours, let's go. In the late afternoon, I saw the wind punch some snow off a moving car. It was beautiful and terrifying, like everything abstract. The sooner you leave, the quicker I won't change my mind. Affection here and there is not enough to bend the cosmos in your favourite direction. There is no hard way to learn, only easy ways. I've been waiting sixty-seven minutes to change for the better.

THE BEE-HERDERS

Why must everything be done

with bells on? said John,

bored as toast, beside a cone-

shaped light.

Start your engines! So I turn

on the shower and it turns

my mind on full. A squid, John said,

is another type of writer

but an abstract kind.

The bees were always less good

than kind, I replied, taking a position.

But in both cases, the anxiety

of doubt and meaninglessness

squeezed back.

I HOPE THIS WILL BE COUNTED SOMEHOW
IN MY DEFENSE

on mornings like this   gusts
play trees against my house

it's a racket

so i let the candle burn right through
the table   and begin to speculate

spirits are always trying to find someone
to live through
from the afterlife

when they do   i'll forget to sweep the house
and need to take a nap

perhaps you'll have found your island by then
and be eating pasta   maybe
you'll have a companion
or some excellent books

i know long ago

i should have gone looking
but instead i spend years
calculating the use

CHAPTER 9

I will doze on the final touch. I will eye the face of the dog. I will be tranquil in Athenian dreams. I will move between countries of darkness. I will command inept attention. I will drown in the pressing wax of children. I will choose the canal of diffidence. I will stay. I will tally my life by mounting into dark.

Also in Parc Lafontaine were several owners and their dogs who then did not take note of the look of disaster which equally tainted my face and manner of walking or stepping and identically affected my twin. Uniquely, we dragged through the park like dogless leashes pulled by some master who too had begun to question what, in fact, had brought him to this park and, moreover, how such sad strings happened to trail his progress in the corner of an April morning in the Plateau. My twin as well as I, together with our memory of the disaster, took up most of an hour despairing that there was nowhere to go from here. Likewise, the paths in the park slowly trailed to a close as infinite ellipses across the hour of six a.m. Comparatively, the disaster was perhaps predictable and, correspondingly, the embarrassment of getting caught within it was similarly predictable. Furthermore, our walk crushingly continued; additionally, l'ennui.

SUBMITTED YET UNSUBMITTED TO UNBENDING LAW

my whole life
i have not been wise

never can tell
if i lost all
or nothing at all

i left the kettle wailing
on the stove
until i burst into flame

but now that i'm older
i can accept the complaints
of that old lady
who lived across the hall

PSALM OF LONELY BREAD

O Lord, give us someone

who can teach me something.

Fill my heart permanently

with the aroma of buttered onions

and lengthen the days of my cat.

Lord, I am only an eater.

I wait in front of my bowlful of peaches.

Hankering every nightfall.

Your morsel-ridden gazer.

And now what? Bring down

the waltzing nameless ones.

Keep me from extra dreaming.

100.

of this beyond all else   I have satisfied myself
man's nature was simple enough when god made him
and these endless questions
are of his own devising

I WAS APPALLED BY THE VISION; I KEPT IT TO MYSELF

what is left unsaid
is an unbest beast

i'm not so easily confused

over the hill   the trees catch fire

and again you let your mind enter
that singular bolt

my dear   a thousand halls will not hold
the procession i've arranged for you

though i wandered out alone
though a lion stood upright
and walked like a man

THE SOMNAMBULIST PARADE

Lord, we always knew you'd be famous. Having been spoon-fed spumoni all our lives. No broken bones. Send your new lover back to the farm and let me refuse another way of seeing. I used such dumb hands to leave the bread crumbs for no one but the thieves.

I am not so happy. Therefore I will take no more photographs. I will loose my onions to some new green arms. My brother's father is dying. I wrote shit lines about hearts. Walk ahead of me, old flames, and I will stalk you back to the station. No one else and no one else and no one else.

Maybe an old man looks for mercies the way a child looks for winks from a stuffed bear. Some things: mercies, a wind across yucky water, another voice not going. No one will answer the full turn, so I stopped paying tribute. Look, I grow to formidable proportions. A desiccated bicycle on an old post slumps in the wake!

Whoever sent that dead rose, listen. Don't keep me so far and long. Give me what I want (the things) and I promise to never lie down again. Don't return to the pond without me. Forget your father's name by the flour mill with your bicycle and jar of sacred almonds. I won't come around. I'll sit in the sycamore. And again.

In the middle of the park (or to the left or right, depending on where you stand), in front of a stone pavilion, being on this side of it and my twin being in the distance (only appearing here and there while I lifted my gaze from the foreground to the background) and what with my twin's geographical position in the park not being central in my mind, while adjacent to the pavilion opposite to my twin, je l'ai perdue. Here was the pavilion and there its other side, but next to its other side at the angle from which I now looked—having gone over to the other side— near the place I assumed my twin to be, my twin was not. I spotted a bridge I had not seen before above the pond and, below it, some loose rock down which one could easily scramble. I approached it and looked under between the loose rock and the underside of the bridge and scrambled down further to see if beyond the arch of the bridge to the shore nearby was perhaps wherever my twin had taken off to. It was now around seven a.m., before many people besides the dog walkers were up, and hence every creature in the park seemed to walk alongside another living or animate being amid the trees that were just beginning to sprout beneath the nerve-wracking false starts of spring. Beside me, on either side, no one. I looked behind once more before I walked across the bridge.

A TOY DEVIL BOBBING IN A TUBE OF CRIMSON BRINE

you get down
to the heart of things
a thorn in this morning's vase
counting ways of being asleep
why not   i am leaving

to find new moons to fill
to pray to the old gods
the broken-down cherry trees
after all

i am only a small dog
in your palm
in the hot air balloon
we are all riding

THE UNPROFESSIONAL CLUB

Someone drew a map of your last aunt's wedding. She held a tiny globe in her hand that bounced. You don't remember how long she wanted a lace to tie her shoe to. She goes out only when the sky is striped. She transgresses dinner with popsicles. Says mercy me at a stain on the ceiling and spends a day watering her shadow. Since then, she has looked for easy words for the hard things. She has a bunch of godmothers to coo to, but the world hasn't changed and no strings snipped. They found her lost sock in a field of Devil's club. So many leftover cousins.

At present, there was insufficient distraction to not think of my twin from time to time and my twin's life, which I knew must sooner or later exist as one apart from mine. At the same time, up to the present time I had perhaps overestimated the nature of our friendship. To begin with, would I have been so quick to disappear? In due time, I'm sure, but until now I had not considered the flightiness of even my own disposition post-disaster. As soon as I considered this, I felt relief that, in the meantime, I would never have to worry about suffering the negative consequences of being responsible for taking off in a moment and without delay. My twin's allegiance to me was, in the first place, sudden, and at this instant did I not wonder, after my twin's disappearance, that I should have predicted such an overzealous attachment would later lead to an overzealous abandonment. Was I the sad dog at last? Until our series of statements or reasons intended to establish either a happy dog or sad dog disposition (and, hence, to refute the opposite) on the Kondiaronk Belvedere, I had not considered that such a perspective would since implicate even me into the categories previously outlined and, placing my singular suffering in the context of a thousand twin sufferers, I shamed myself that, before this, I had not considered what was perhaps "dans les cartes."

OAKS AND PLAINS

Lord, you fill my nose with the scent

of cut grass and move the water

by my feet in one direction only.

The fire you depend on

is hot and good. In it, I make my way

to new bones. Rub the salve

with your everlasting thumb.

If you wanted us to follow

your spirit, why did you give it

so many perches? Something else must want

to sling along the treetops.

CHAPTER 10

What is the final touch going to do? What is the fabulous city going to be? Where am I going to find a milling neighbour? When is the full light going to be cut off? The vital bog sunk in restless memory? Who is going to eye the unborn birds? When is the world going to have turned enough? When is the abominable wind going to leave us to our hung sleep? When am I going to sink totally into the broken web of earth? Enter tranquil nighthood? The thought, merely lately.

NOT THE LAST JUDGEMENT, JUST A KERMESS
BY A RIVER

finally   i heard your voice
riding on a tropical breeze
only you had a name for

tell me of the island
i asked   where you became a ray of light
where your crutched heart
leapt like a deer

no one else is found there
no drunkards   not the dead
it said

just you
mute-tongued
shouting for joy   .

THE TRIUMPHANT EXIT

The raising of our pet dog

is a recent example of

all the miracles. Lord,

I must stay at your house.

Let's make a camp far away

from the fiery lakes

and sulphur tornadoes.

Away from that self-portrait.

Where that sycamore went

I wonder, drinking

the pink lemon water.

I have seen so much,

do I really have to see any more?

Hence, I forthwith continued my wander since there was no object in looking for someone when that someone chose not to be found, and to look once around the pavilion and under the bridge was more than enough. I straightaway went about leaving the park not knowing where next to go but meanwhile facing the terrible resolve to, henceforth, go alone. Whenever I encounter terrible firmness or steadfastness of purpose, determination, or an instance of this, I eventually drive myself into such a pit of "doute de soi" that the walk and the motion of going further into both the physical and psychological unknown during an aftermath of a disaster (which first leashed me to an uncertain fate, and second lost my twin just in time to instigate confusion prior to my revelation that perhaps it was not some uncertain fate) are rendered meaningless.

PSALM OF A HUNDREDTH PART OF A GIFT

Let down the plumb line,

Lord. I'll run its distance.

I am overwritten

on your papers.

My feet are on the sill.

An exhale of smoke

was a weird message to send me.

Still, I dip my hand into its jar.

Walk myself home.

WHAT HAD TO BE A SHAME

mouth full of stale candy
tub love song   run out   run out

always drinking the worst wine
worse to write about it

come to my house
full of never-night

corner-sunk light
holy apple left darkening

I left me
sitting here   nothing-doing

rerise
i will hunch in the small bowl

with the dregs   the future-
telling kind

THE WORLD HATES TOO MUCH FIRE

Garden me, Lord, and remain

for me to bear with you.

Let me ask what I wish:

for glory, etc.

If I lose my friend, how can I mourn

for him your way?

I am still young at resurrection.

No one comes out.

I'm tired of yelling at graves.

I am the worst at drawing fruit.

A friend calls me,

says, Geez, come on.

Either my twin left willingly or not. As soon as these thoughts settled, just as I breached the muddy edge of the park onto Rue Rachel, I regretted my disdain, which was both petty and unjustified. Well, neither possibility could solve the dilemma nor restore to me my twin who had not only vanished but left no trace. Not only was I now alone, but because of this state or quality of being solitary, I decided it was best to begin to forget. Immediately, quickly, finally, I denied what thoughts I had of my twin to release myself from the ghost of my twin (who formerly existed and suddenly disappeared) and shortly I discovered that all thoughts of this past twin could not instantly evaporate and I presently gave up, trying instead to render my thinking of my twin at all as "comme ci, comme ça" at best. For if my walk continued and my twin did not return, I could remove neither my twin's memory from the routes we travelled together nor the memories of conversations triggered by certain landmarks along said routes but rather would have to suffer being hounded by the aforementioned memories or else stop walking completely, yet the prospect of someone having the power to render another legless due to the complex and multiple conjunctions of conversation, thought, memory, history, geography, anatomy, incident, and disaster that occur during what seems a simple physical movement, one foot at a time from one place to another, was too outrageous to bear, despite its accuracy. One either walks or one doesn't. Happy...sad? Alas, the same dog.

OLD DREAM OF A VOLCANIC DESERT

past the palm trees   a sail
boat feeding on oceans
of misuse   a presumable island
a rickety fence   fantasy lighthouse

i want to be buried in wood   so?
the nearest shore laps in the mind
the real frontier
no wars to speak of

i put my sunglasses on the table
like i mean it   i keep them there
no   i probably won't
marry you   cheers to this beer   that won't be our last
but should be

WHERE IS THE HOUSE YOU WILL BUILD FOR ME?

There were three opposites

in the wetland museum.

Items relating to the heavens—

the taxidermied and the unremarkable.

Embalm me, with my tusks

hung low. Keep me from public view.

Lifelike, but rather.

Strangest stranger.

Fulfill your schemes, lay out

the science and the ethics,

the elephant foot,

in case I miss something.

THE WORD PAST DOES NOT MEAN ANYTHING

they filled your cup with leaves
you bring me a bottle of your grandfather's port

the kindest have learned to keep distance
the saddest cover my face with their hair

who knew the dodo was a crow?
long black neck beneath

long black sun

WHO SHALL KEEP MY SHEEP?

My Lord, you have honeyed

the bread of life. Lit a holy candle

far enough away from the dry flowers.

Give me your love, and help me

gather it up.

Praise the Lord, soul my O.

The trees are watered with the wine

of the bad kids. The leviathan

is hosting your heavenlies

and bidding your dos. The birds

have branched among your singing

and everywhere, dominion cedars.

My Lord, you have breaded

the honey. Dried the holy flowers

and made a trail of seasons

through the desert. Give me your help

and love me gather it up. Your open hand

has been for so long.

RETINUES OF HOMESPUN VELVETEEN SKIRTS

tell me if it is too far for you
and i will tell you to run
past those fields   down the ridge
but not too seriously

and if you dream of an archipelago
turn down the thick streets
soon i will be there

i'll keep it until then

till the tracks of coyotes
and the mule deer bend towards the pond
that could have held you
above its waters

CHAPTER 11

I will be fully sinking. I will be praying to the narrowest tunnels. I will be spelling my name in blades of grass. I will be interrupting no one. I will be opting for foxes to further me on. I will be kneeling unseen. I will be peeking on my fall's flight. I will not be calling to stop. I will be purely staying. I will be seeing my grave as blue. I will not be fearing. I will be running myself under. I will be one time seeming foamly. I will be travelling not. Done flight. Dumb flight.

PSALM OF NO MORE MARIGOLDS PLEASE

and the problem is   the fall cut   the hung pine
my ears burnt with your radiance
not knowing the streets you've walked me down

come on now   start at the top of the glass

send along that friendly smile you promised
am i not waiting in the daisies?
i can't remember if i think or
don't think i understand your struggle
the game's played out of earshot

when you dared me to dive in
i didn't think you would

doddering in your drunken flight
to the corner of the restaurant

we will move below the clouds
or they will move above us   you said
i guess

when i call   sometimes
you answer   that's enough

In short, when my twin did reappear in brief three days later near the pavilion in Parc Lafontaine, my twin had so changed in countenance that to summarize the differences here would be impossible. To put the two on balance would put the balancer in such a state of shock that he or she would altogether not believe that my twin and my twin's new countenance were overall that of the same twin. Ordinarily, disasters do not result in such transfigurations and usually the wilfully disappeared do not return so conspicuously. By and large we found the whole thing frankly ridiculous and, to sum up our opinion on the matter of walks, disasters, dogs, and the like, we, on the whole, are beginning to think a piece of writing or an oral composition about said things in which the expression of feelings or ideas is typically given intensity and flavour by distinctive diction, rhythm, imagery, etc., would be a faux pas. In any event, it is hard enough for us to adjust to my twin's new countenance—in either case!—either as the one inhabiting the new skin or the other ogling. The discomfort of recording it would not be worth the risk to our already fragile state of mind and, to be frank, the probability of anyone believing in a person's sudden transfiguration under the context of having simply decided to go for a walk (which is both conducive to a] avoiding disaster and b] strengthening one's anatomy) is, in the end, absurd.

CHAPTER 12

I'll have relaxed in defeat. I will have no wit to be afraid. I'll have returned as a stray to the fold. I'll have honeyed the season's dusk. I'll have applauded the theatre of air. I'll have belled without voice. I'll have stood still for many weeks. I'll have strove not to desert nor be deserted. I'll have been all-returned to soil. I'll have snowed as colour. I'll have strung my hopes limb-high in the iris of the sun, where the dead winter will have unconceded to remain near its beginning. In its numb foreign poetry, combly and frail, I will have left.

SLAMMED CUPBOARD ONE NIGHT LONG AGO LONG AGO NOW

ages ago had been the first time
rattling its tusks into the gorgeous night

you make me spaghetti
and i stop giving you commands

taken to taking my friend's advice
keeping it all at bay

why we hadn't thought of this earlier
it was about distillation

the new hadn't been the right one
pitter patter

*

come home
i'll be your together

i thought i heard the behind your eyes
never coming too close

the theme of my life was comets
running into you

outside your new home
startling   to say the least

it wasn't that it didn't give us meaning
but that the meaning was withheld

a cramp in the meat of the palm
a false enthusiasm

the last few moments of it
the train   taking over

YOU'RE THE FINDER

There's a cloud full

in the hold of the sky. John said,

if you learn to love a thing,

you need it longer.

You've got it all:

two hands, a grandfather mug,

official permission, and

ordained mingling.

Frequent loss of the courage

to be in it; the lord of that

stirring, the incomprehensible

inkwells in the accusing

of myself.

YOUR BIRTHDAY IS MY BIRTHDAY

for B.H.

i keep house casually

a bookshelf of blue paintings
and some empty picture frames

i ran out to the sound of your footsteps by my home
and returned   but while i was gone
someone hid the whisky

there were nights we walked to the water
but something ran ahead

turn your face
the water   dearest friend

from this angle
could be the ocean

THE HUMAN TRADITION

It was in your best interests to tell a story the human way. Hadn't you always known? Saving plates for imaginary arguments, all in your garbage palace.

You've decided to enter the grave slowly. Watch the rebellion take place on a room temperature field. Lay me down above a magic keyhole. Tell the dragons and the pregnant women. But the kind of despair described in ____ was over one's head.

When I am an old man, eating toast with ketchup, I will give myself a few years to think over things.

THE UNHAD BACKYARD

One. The palm head rester. Two. The dead horse under the mound, greened over. Three. Making tea from weeds. Four. My sister, flight. Five. The glasses, thick so. Precious pink hooks of them. Ear-wrapping. Precious. Your little ears. The poised paw shape of them. The too much of them.

In a manner of speaking, I am come over. Tethered to the scope, breath-held. Heart full of loose hairs. Swept with them. No cards to bear, in a manner of speaking. In a manner of speaking, I am unpeaceful. Sister, have at me. In a manner unspeaking. The arcane scales of it, my dragon. The gross weight of it, my butterfly.

City where I am. You're around the lake again, freezing. Hail, I am at the foot of your pond. Hail, I am at the foot of your hill. Hail, the small mountain. Sister. I am at the foot of your bed, flayed as a hawk tail. Hail, the broken arm of you. Hail, the too small socks. Sister, I am sorry. As the light on the face of the building facing the sun set years ago, where I am.

Hang me in your house, straight as the blinds. I am your oldest protector. Don't leave me at the top of your stairs again. Sister, come home, littler this time. I will send moving horses beside your trip. Change your season and I'll make a sandwich in your name. Send before you your birds who are moths, and I will receive them. They will fill my cupboards. They are your questions, setting over me. I'll love you in their dusk. I shall not waste them.

YOU LOOK COOL IN YOUR EAGLE SUIT

PART I: THE MASK

Nothing comes, and if it does, it is nothing. No one has mercy on it.
Been merciful only to somethings.

—Anonymous

Chapter 1

Your heart, poised in its rib accordion, did not mind being free.
"Do not mind being free, rib heart," it said. You listened, but were
distracted by the corn chips, which were blue. "Just listen," said the
colour blue, "there is a door to a place known by most people who've
passed through it." You were at the door's corner.

Chapter 2

Lord, life is not easy without your hill metaphors. It was nice to
find on my shelf the unused plastic beer cup. You came to paint the
ceiling the light had broken, then went for a soaky walk. "Don't mind
being free," said.

Chapter 3

It took too much time: the constant everywhere-glancing.
Hunched in denim, ponyless, aflame in bitter mercies. "Take me
somewhere good," say. A hung sun thumbing light across sand. A
trip to gorgeous postcards.

Chapter 4

Sit and make of things with me. The windows stay in their orange tracks all night. No one told me the right way to sit on a balcony. Or if the hovering lump of stones on the building's face will fall on me while I sit.

Chapter 5

Twin, you are in America or Paris or something. I am beneath the stones. I am drawing unsanctimonious circles around me. I removed the hair from my drink. I am blameless.

Chapter 6

Dear twin. Having known little of you. The bell-lift of your voice is on the hem of my steps. I am on life's knee. What it hasn't been is always more interesting. A phone call not going through. Someone in the soaked alley instead of me. Another unresolved resolve. Pretending to see you to see you.

Chapter 7

My life: bad at unchoosing. "Dear mouth, is this please the last time I shall hear you?" A flower blooms in a forest, and sees no one. Dusk recurs. It rerains, and I delete myself inside a wine-sphere. "Hey! the floor!" my last mouth says. The sky is a speculation. The sky speculates.

PART II

You learn from your mistakes. You will learn a lot today.
    —Christian Horoscope

Chapter 8

It was a good thing to take that hand, all those years ago. Being unable to walk, it's a good thing you took that hand. What are the chances of the sky falling right on the tip of you? What are the chances of you asking? Your sobriety is the elegance of every flamingo standing at once the same way. You are the birds' noses, pointed one direction. I've counted fourteen types of weather on my pen.

Chapter 9

I am walking you across the street. You are a small, irritable animal that wears shoes. I tried to put them on, but they were just balloons with their stems cut off.

Chapter 10

Is that you now coming back? You tell me to take my paradise seafoam dream to the other side of the popsicle stand. Come over so I can tell you I like the way you write your name down. The slow unfoldingishness of it.

Chapter 11

Whatever form it took, the way the hat froze your do was a still wind-sweep. I can't wait a second longer, so I reach into the brown bag, and a piece appears. It reminds me of another piece. One I ate with you years ago, or was it days later, on this very corner, on a move towards another corner.

Chapter 12

When I tell people stories you tell me, they sound more like charms. Yes, I am morningish, if that's what you meant. Maybe I shouldn't give you all my money, but it brings me that security feeling.

Chapter 13

I am not your backyard, but I'm having a swell time watching you. I am full of power — watch out. You might walk by, and I might call you by your first name, the one we all know. I gave you mine, that time, so you could remember it.

Chapter 14

The end might come and there you'll be. Cursing my doorsill, drinking two too many. Minding. Not minding. Remember: the marshmallows floated in the hot chocolate like undemoted planets. If there's a wait, I'll be at the end of it. Come home, twin. Venice doesn't need you anymore. There's a person sitting alone on its balcony, becoming inhospitable to it. We may be eternal, but we'll never know. I've already consumed much to make me feel endish.

PART III

I am trying to understand your very important meanings.
    —Anonymous

Chapter 15

This is not its own, but the roads are the same. The alleys, exactly the same. It's just mine that has been changing. Sometimes I ask, is this the same? And put all my processes to a halt till it's gone. Well, I only speak in terms of them anyway.

Chapter 16

Your hunger was a giveaway. I was a pesticide fruit stand. You were the dust off coloured chalk in the wind, hanging sierra nevadas in my mind. Who will sit beside me now? I wonder who will sit there.

Chapter 17

Hand me an apron and a can of mace, I know the tricks. I'll pass them down generations. Sorry I'm a mean drunk, but you are far and long, and I'm still sitting in the Arizona desert, alone. A gun wasn't the best thing to leave me with. I could use food, water. Stuck with ale, nothing doing, trying to cover up the look. Hey, sunkish whales, make your pretty arches in my ocean. I won't boat around anymore. I don't boat. Singing underwater. Imagining nextness.

Chapter 18

The wings made loud, anarchic noises. They styro by and
I am possessed by many bones. Okay, I'll stay on the mountain.
Get the way you told me. Stabbed like a flag in the nouveau
territory, somewhere in the spoken-of forest. Uncuddlish, as always.
Waving back. Mortifying my sisters. Their hands full of spoons they
wanted to feed me with.

Chapter 19

The crests of seafoam adorn your Hawaiian tees like your
accent, your true self. You look for grapes to make juice with. At
parties, put the shrimp ring in just the right spot. I didn't want it.
I didn't have time.

Chapter 20

Hey, whale song, bellow me a hopeful note. I am stuck running
through my desert's childhood, putting off my very important work
of finding my way out. Ungladding what I have. Watching it.

Chapter 21

I am the one who sits and sits. All I wanted were more sizes to
be in. Not these feast scraps. You are the one who heads for the sea.
You send me photos of your shrimp shells, your porch covered in
flowers. Vines, roses, jades, avocado trees. I gave you the one
I'd grown.

PART IV

At the place where I am always at, I am asked to take it into my arms.
I do. I don't know it well enough to use certain words.
    —Anonymous, a long time ago

Chapter 22

You are rewarded by my leaving you. I am small on the turret. I
have my own at my own feet.

Chapter 23

I am just the dweller. Wanting more sizes to be in.

Chapter 24

It was a finishing question. I had crept to the other side of the
bench of it. I had put my name on the list of it. In speaking, I became
the I of you. Let me go of it.

Chapter 25

If I had known failure, I would have practiced more. I transcend
the side streets by thinking of them. Every place, full of it. I'm sorry I
lit the stained-glass windows. Illuminating it. Puking the meal of it.

Chapter 26

Milk of the stars. Where you slept last night. A door shuts behind me and I am left in the midst of you. A hand finds me in the middle of the night. I hold it. I imitate. The many life tales of this. Tin cans behind the wasted truck.

Chapter 27

Dear twin. I would like to pass my life right-doing, but you have broken my door.

Chapter 28

Dear twin. I write in your language the things I try to mean.

Chapter 29

Dear twin. The sad things you do to me.

Chapter 30

Dear twin. I will play the piano over you.

Chapter 31

Dear twin. I will follow you with the longest poem.

Chapter 32

Dear twin. I will not come to easily.

Chapter 33

Dear twin. I will attend.

Chapter 34

Dear twin. If I were like you.

Chapter 35

Dear twin. If you were like me.

Chapter 36

Dear twin. Did we not both stand under it?

Chapter 37

Dear twin. I lost the word that was looking for me.

Chapter 38

Dear twin. So much ash to be blessed.

Chapter 39

Dear twin. I am won by silence. The mudsucker under the lake.

Chapter 40

Dear twin. Shoot up the geyser.

Chapter 41

Dear twin. My hair turns white but I dye it stone.

Chapter 42

Dear twin. On both hands, you are.

Chapter 43

Dear twin.

Chapter 44

Where my heart is.

Chapter 45

Twin,

Chapter 46

There is no difference between the unknown of me and the known of you.

NOTES

Some of the titles in this manuscript are borrowed lines from Czeslaw Milosz and can be found in *Czeslaw Milosz: Selected and Last Poems 1931–2004* (Ecco, 2006).

The list poem that starts with the title "for i believed in the existence of a last door" is made up of various official translations of Ecclesiastes 7:29.

The first line of "your birthday is my birthday" is a reference to Kobayashi Issa.

"with a flick of my wrist, i fashioned an invisible rope, and climbed it and it held me" uses 150 English prepositions, which is most of them.

"that chase with the hounds for the unattainable meaning of the world" is structured on the use of English conjunctions and transitional phrases. Excluding the first page, all pages include (a) a reference to a street or landmark in Montréal, (b) a reference to a dog or doglike feature, and (c) an embedded *Oxford English Dictionary* definition. An earlier version of this poem appeared as a chapbook with Proper Tales Press in November 2013 under the title "Happy Dog, Sad Dog." The whole poem is based on a misunderstanding (on my part) about a limping dog. I apologize to my walking partner.

A selection of the poems in this manuscript appear in a chapbook with Baseline Press under the title "Love the Sacred Raisins Cakes."

Another selection of the poems in this manuscript appear in a chapbook with above/ground press under the title "A Precarious Life on the Sea."

"an eagle flew in the sun again but it didn't mean the same" was turned into a musical score by composer JP Merz and performed in Middlebury, Vermont, at the New Music on the Point Festival, June 2015. A recording can be found here: www.jpmerz.com.

"Fessin for the Monarch" appeared in *Illiterature*, Issue 2014.

"The Astrologer Showdown" and "Particular Hexes" appeared in *Matrix Magazine*'s 100th Issue, 2014.

"Love, Please Do So at the Self" appeared in *THIS Magazine*, Summer 2014.

"Who Shall Keep My Sheep?," "Anointing My Own Head with My Own Oil," "The Mighty Ones Are Budding," and "At the Potter's House" appeared in *The Capilano Review*, Languages Issue, Spring 2014.

"Bippity" appears in *Used Gravitrons*, Issue 18, Winter 2014.

ACKNOWLEDGEMENTS

Thanks to Stuart for meeting me in the kingdom of music. Thanks, Paul and Sue, for filling my heart cafeteria with millions. Thanks, Emily, Blythe and Sophie, for being supernatural brothers. Thanks, Irene, for noticing the aphids. Thanks to the eternal spaghetti of my Friday friends! (Holy Nick holy Hilary holy Will holy Kyl holy Paige holy Yann holy the unknown Eloise!) Thanks, Stephanie Bolster, for the extra-brilliant intelligent kindness of your soul. Thanks, Sina Queyras, Gail Scott, Mary di Michele, Andre Furlani, Lorna Crozier, Steven Price, Carla Funk, and Tim Lilburn, for raising me in poetry and filling my brain with a heaventree of stars. Thanks, Donna Kane, for the flaming bulrushes. Thanks, H.N., for the twin clocks in space. Thanks, Charls Osaniah, for crazy Tuesdays, in particular. Thanks, Sue Sinclair, Nick Thran, and Abby, for the happy hunting ground of your minds. Thanks, Liam Sarsfield, for the bagel days. Thanks, Karen Schindler, for the editing, publishing, and generous hosting! Thanks, rob mclennan, for the same. And thanks again to Stuart, who first published a poem of mine that outed me on falling in love with everyone. I am beside the pond with all of you.

Sarah Burgoyne grew up in B.C., where she has lived in Vancouver, Langley, Victoria, and the small community of Princeton. She currently resides in Montreal, where she studied at Concordia University. She has published four chapbooks, including *Love the Sacred Raisin Cakes* (Baseline Press) and *Happy Dog, Sad Dog* (Proper Tales Press), and has been shortlisted for the Montreal Poetry Prize. She teaches at Dawson College. *Saint Twin* is her first full-length poetry collection.

Other Books From Mansfield Press

Poetry

Leanne Averbach, *Fever*
Tara Azzopardi, *Last Stop, Lonesome Town*
Nelson Ball, *Chewing Water*
Nelson Ball, *In This Thin Rain*
Nelson Ball, *Some Mornings*
Gary Barwin, *Moon Baboon Canoe*
George Bowering, *Teeth: Poems 2006–2011*
Stephen Brockwell, *Complete Surprising Fragments of Improbable Books*
Stephen Brockwell & Stuart Ross, eds., *Rogue Stimulus: The Stephen Harper Holiday Anthology for a Prorogued Parliament*
Diana Fitzgerald Bryden, *Learning Russian*
Alice Burdick, *Book of Short Sentences*
Alice Burdick, *Flutter*
Alice Burdick, *Holler*
Jason Camlot, *What The World Said*
Margaret Christakos, *wipe.under.a.love*
Pino Coluccio, *First Comes Love*
Marie-Ève Comtois, *My Planet of Kites*
Dani Couture, *YAW*
Gary Michael Dault, *The Milk of Birds*
Frank Davey, *Poems Suitable to Current Material Conditions*
Pier Giorgio Di Cicco, *The Dark Time of Angels*
Pier Giorgio Di Cicco, *Dead Men of the Fifties*
Pier Giorgio Di Cicco, *The Honeymoon Wilderness*
Pier Giorgio Di Cicco, *Living in Paradise*
Pier Giorgio Di Cicco, *Early Works*
Pier Giorgio Di Cicco, *The Visible World*
Salvatore Difalco, *What Happens at Canals*
Christopher Doda, *Aesthetics Lesson*
Christopher Doda, *Among Ruins*
Glen Downie, *Monkey Soap*
Rishma Dunlop, *The Body of My Garden*
Rishma Dunlop, *Lover Through Departure: New and Selected Poems*
Rishma Dunlop, *Metropolis*
Rishma Dunlop & Priscila Uppal, eds., *Red Silk: An Anthology of South Asian Women Poets*
Ollivier Dyens, *The Profane Earth*
Laura Farina, *Some Talk of Being Human*
Jaime Forsythe, *Sympathy Loophole*
Carole Glasser Langille, *Late in a Slow Time*
Eva HD, *Rotten Perfect Mouth*
Eva HD, *Wolverine States*
Suzanne Hancock, *Another Name for Bridge*
Jason Heroux, *Emergency Hallelujah*
Jason Heroux, *Hard Work Cheering Up Sad Machines*
Jason Heroux, *Memoirs of an Alias*
Jason Heroux, *Natural Capital*
John B. Lee, *In the Terrible Weather of Guns*
Jeanette Lynes, *The Aging Cheerleader's Alphabet*
David W. McFadden, *Abnormal Brain Sonnets*
David W. McFadden, *Be Calm, Honey*
David W. McFadden, *Shouting Your Name Down the Well: Tankas and Haiku*

David W. McFadden, *What's the Score?*
Kathryn Mockler, *The Purpose Pitch*
Leigh Nash, *Goodbye, Ukulele*
Lillian Necakov, *The Bone Broker*
Lillian Necakov, *Hooligans*
Peter Norman, *At the Gates of the Theme Park*
Peter Norman, *Water Damage*
Natasha Nuhanovic, *Stray Dog Embassy*
Catherine Owen & Joe Rosenblatt, *Dog*
Corrado Paina, *The Alphabet of the Traveler*
Corrado Paina, *Cinematic Taxi*
Corrado Paina, *The Dowry of Education*
Corrado Paina, *Hoarse Legend*
Corrado Paina, *Souls in Plain Clothes*
Nick Papaxanthos, *Love Me Tender*
Stuart Ross et al., *Our Days in Vaudeville*
Matt Santateresa, *A Beggar's Loom*
Matt Santateresa, *Icarus Redux*
Ann Shin, *The Last Thing Standing*
Jim Smith, *Back Off, Assassin! New and Selected Poems*
Jim Smith, *Happy Birthday, Nicanor Parra*
Robert Earl Stewart, *Campfire Radio Rhapsody*
Robert Earl Stewart, *Something Burned on the Southern Border*
Carey Toane, *The Crystal Palace*
Aaron Tucker, *Punchlines*
Priscila Uppal, *Sabotage*
Priscila Uppal, *Summer Sport: Poems*
Priscila Uppal, *Winter Sport: Poems*
Steve Venright, *Floors of Enduring Beauty*
Brian Wickers, *Stations of the Lost*

Fiction

Marianne Apostolides, *The Lucky Child*
Sarah Dearing, *The Art of Sufficient Conclusions*
Denis De Klerck, ed., *Particle & Wave: A Mansfield Omnibus of Electro-Magnetic Fiction*
Salvatore Difalco, *Mean Season*
Paula Eisenstein, *Flip Turn*
Sara Heinonen, *Dear Leaves, I Miss You All*
Christine Miscione, *Carafola*
Marko Sijan, *Mongrel*
Tom Walmsley, *Dog Eat Rat*
Corinne Wasilewski, *Live from the Underground*

Non-Fiction

George Bowering, *How I Wrote Certain of My Books*
Denis De Klerck & Corrado Paina, eds., *College Street–Little Italy: Toronto's Renaissance Strip*
Pier Giorgio Di Cicco, *Municipal Mind: Manifestos for the Creative City*
Amy Lavender Harris, *Imagining Toronto*
David W. McFadden, *Mother Died Last Summer*
Deborah Verginella, ed., *Buon Appetito Toronto!*

For a complete list of Mansfield Press titles, please visit mansfieldpress.net